Dinghy helming

Dinghy helming
Lawrie Smith

photographs by Tim Hore

Fernhurst Books

First published 1983 by
Fernhurst Books, 13 Fernhurst Road, London SW6 7JN

ISBN 0 906754 09 7

Acknowledgements

The publishers would like to thank Mark Simpson and Ossie Stewart who
crewed for the photographs. Thanks are also due to Queen Mary Sailing
Club, Ashford, Middlesex and Parkstone Yacht Club, Poole, Dorset for
their assistance during the photo sessions.

The photographs on pages 21 and 43 are reproduced with kind per-
mission of Performance Sailcraft (UK) Ltd. The photographs on pages 38,
62 and the cover are by Kos, and the cover design is by Behram Kapadia.

Composition by Allset, London
Printed by Butler & Tanner Ltd, Frome

Contents

Introduction

Before the start of any campaign you must decide how successful you want to be and to what lengths you are prepared to go to achieve this success. If you are already a good club helmsman* sailing every weekend, you may only need to improve your techniques slightly to be in the top 15 at your National Championships. If, however, you want to be National Champion, you must put a great deal more time and effort into gaining your objective. So, decide first what your aim is and whether it is possible to commit enough time and finance to achieve it.

One of the most difficult tasks is assessing your own potential, because if you do not have some natural talent it will be very hard to win a National title in one of the big popular classes. Having said that, don't despair — anybody who spends sufficient time and money will not be very far from the number one spot if he or she goes about the job in the right way.

Assuming you have decided to win the National title in your class, you must have the following resources:

1   A first-class crew who is the correct weight and size for the boat, is fit and agile, has sufficient racing experience and the time and money to support himself for the duration of the campaign.

2   A boat and equipment at least as good as any rival's

3   Time and finance to support a long season of racing, sailing every weekend, plus two nights a week, and at least four weeks per season.

4   Enough races under your belt to give you a good feel for strategy, tactics and the rules.

If you can achieve all these, the rest is determination, effort — and the skills outlined in this book.

Part one of this book explains the techniques you must master during your practice sessions. The objective is to show you how to make the boat go as fast as possible in all conditions of wind and sea. For most of the manoeuvres I describe first how to handle the boat in medium winds and then show how to modify this for light and heavy airs.

Part two looks at the race itself and how you can apply your helming skills to win.

How large an improvement should you be looking for? The difference in distance between twentieth place and first place in most major championships is very small, usually 200 to 300 yards. Therefore you need only improve your performance by a fraction of one per cent to gain twenty places. Don't look for overnight success by simply buying new sails or boats, but work at the finer points and, eventually, you will edge your way towards the front. There is no magic formula, only a lot of painstaking work with boat and crew, gradually eliminating errors, improving techniques and bringing the boat to its best for the big week. For instance, go out and practise mark rounding and tacking — if you can improve each tack so you lose only two yards instead of three you have already gained twenty yards at the end of an Olympic course.

*Publisher's note: "or helmswoman" is implied throughout.

Part 1
Helming techniques

1 Beating

Beating in medium winds

Conditions. Flat open water, 6 to 15 knots of wind, and the best boat and rig available.

Objectives. To make the best VMG (velocity made good) to the weather mark. You are out to find the best compromise between speed through the water and pointing ability.

The rig. In these conditions the boat must be pointing as close to the wind as possible. There are no waves to stop you and speed is easily achieved and maintained; therefore sails must be set reasonably flat with a small amount of twist. The mainsail is sheeted with the aft end of the boom 2 inches off the centreline and the jib set on its innermost fairlead position. Standing rigging must be tight: 300 to 350 lb on the luff

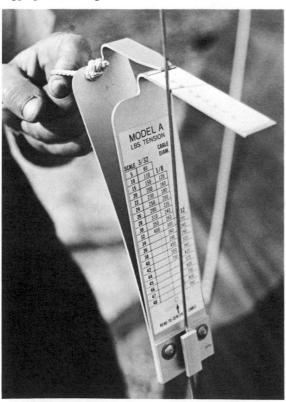

wire inside the jib is ideal for most classes. Pull the foot of the mainsail out to the black band to flatten the lower third of the sail.

Boat trim. The boat at all times must be kept absolutely level: anything other than a slight heel to windward will slow you down. If the boat does heel, everything starts working against you.

1   The centreboard will be less efficient if it is not vertical.

2   The air will be diverted and disturbed by flowing over the topsides of the hull before it reaches the lower sections of the sails.

3   In almost all dinghy classes the hull is designed to be more efficient when level. This gives maximum waterline length, and is particularly important in non-planing conditions.

4   The heel of the boat will create too much weather helm, making the rudder act as a brake.

Before attempting to sail the boat upright you first have to learn the technique. Most sailors believe their boats are level when in fact they are still heeled 5° or 10°. The best way to perfect the technique is to go out and practise on your own, looking backwards and lining the top two corners of the transom with the water. This will give you a good indication of your sideways trim, as will studying the flow of water off the stern of the boat. You will see a disturbance off the leeward quarter if you are heeled.

For correct fore and aft trim, the helm and crew must be as close together as possible, the crew's back foot or (if not trapezing) body touching the helmsman, leaving only enough room for the movement of his mainsheet arm. The crew's forward foot should be positioned 9 to 12 inches behind the shroud, the idea being to keep maximum waterline length and to stop the stern digging. Also if the bow is too far out of the water it will tend to get blown away from the wind and pointing will suffer.

Left: a tension device is a vital aid to tuning. Use it to measure the rig tension when you achieve good speed so you can repeat the settings.

Beating in medium winds. Above: the boat is well balanced
with helm and crew positioned for maximum speed. Right:
the effect of heel is to increase weather helm (note the tiller
angle) and drag from the leeward quarter (shown by the
quarter wave).

Centreboard. In these conditions it pays to angle the
board 5° forward. This helps to point closer to the
wind by moving the centre of effort forwards. The
reason for moving the board is so that the mast
doesn't have to be raked excessively to induce enough
weather helm when the boat is upright. Of course, if
the boat is allowed to heel then you will have too
much.

Mainsheet, traveller and vang.   The sail must be kept
reasonably flat with little twist, so providing there are
no frequent large gusts the traveller should be adjusted
rather than the mainsheet. 'Playing' the mainsheet to
control the angle of the boom on its horizontal
plane would require vang tension; vang tension
reduces power in the mainsail by over-bending the
lower half of the mast and opening the top of the
mainsail. Therefore the vang must be slack.

Tiller and rudder. The tiller extension must be long enough for you to be able to steer while sitting up against the shroud in light winds. Any longer or shorter is no good. When sitting on the deck (as against hiking out) it is better to hold the tiller by your side, otherwise the tip of the extension will become tied up in the mainsheet. When hiking hold it in front of you so that you can use your tiller hand on the mainsheet when adjusting the vang, cunningham, etc.

Rudder movements should never be excessive as you are not forcing the boat down a wave or trying to promote planing. Accurate and sensitive movements are the best, steering the straightest and shortest course according to changes in the wind.

Cunningham. As a rule, never use the cunningham unless overpowered. It bends the mast and opens the top of the mainsail, reducing power. Don't worry about the horizontal creases running out of the luff behind the mast.

Steering. Pointing and speed are related. If you are going slowly but pointing high you may appear to be going in a good direction but you will also be making more leeway then someone who is not pointing as high but going faster. It is, therefore, very important to achieve maximum speed before trying to point. You should have telltales on the luff of the jib at one-third, half, and two-thirds luff length. Get all these streaming, with the weather ones just beginning to 'break', then steer as accurately as possible to them. Your mainsail should have a telltale or streamer positioned on the very back of the leech,

Above: hold the tiller extension in front of you when hiking so you can use your tiller hand on the mainsheet if required. Opposite, left: the correct mainsail setting for medium winds. The boom is 2 inches off the centreline, no cunningham (don't worry about the luff creases) and just the right amount of twist. The boat is also nicely upright. Right: too much cunningham opens the upper leech and gives too much twist. The boom is too far out and the boat is heeling.

just under the top batten. Sheet the mainsail until this is just beginning to break. Keep the boat level and keep her going fast!

Gusts and lulls. In medium winds your crew should always be trapezing, even if this means you have to sit on the deck rather than hike. The benefits are:

1 Extra support for the mast (more power).

2 Better vision for helm and crew.

3 Trapezing enables the helm and crew to get closer together, with the crew's back foot behind the helmsman.

4 The crew can stretch or bend very quickly to the changes in the wind speed.

As soon as the wind will support him your crew should be out on the trapeze wire. Trapezing high will help him get out sooner. As a gust hits, the crew is the first to move, extending himself outwards to counteract the extra pressure. If this is not sufficient he should lower himself using the trapeze adjuster. Finally he can put his arms behind his head to produce more leverage. Meanwhile the helmsman should ease his bodyweight over the side while at the same time hardening closer to the wind and releasing the traveller

down its track to reduce power and keep the boat level. If the gust looks like being permanent, then mainsail and jib will have to be sheeted in harder to compensate.

In a lull, the first to move is the helmsman who should come in from the hiked position. If you are not hiking, then the crew should raise himself back higher on the trapeze and then bend his knees, not his back. At the same time, both sheets should be eased, and the traveller reset.

Concentration. Concentration at all times must be 100 per cent. Anything short of this will result in your losing speed or missing a shift. The more you practise the easier it becomes; you are trying to make fast sailing second nature. Try not to get too tense or nervous as this will make you stiff and clumsy around the boat, gripping the tiller too hard or pulling the mainsheet in too tight. Attention must be paid to setting your sails correctly — once again, with practice this becomes much easier. Watching telltales and trim is important, but there is no substitute for time on the water to give a complete feel for the boat, and you should be able to steer to within 2° or 3° of the wind with your eyes closed. When you can do this you can then concentrate more on shifts, compass and your competitors.

You and your crew should always have a note of the compass readings on both tacks. If you do get a header then wait for four or five seconds before tacking to make sure it is a genuine shift.

Going slowly. Common mistakes are:

1 Oversheeting of sails.

2 Making sails too full to create more power.

3 Thinking you are going slowly when in fact boats around are in a different wind or are, in reality, no faster than you.

Non-trapeze boats. In most classes of two-man dinghy the above principles apply. In the Enterprise class the rule prevents you from sheeting the jib close enough to the centreline, forcing you to have a very flat sail which must then be sheeted much harder and never eased more than 2 inches. Mainsails are also much fuller because of the wider slot, and need to be sheeted further outboard 4 to 5 inches off the centreline.

Correct mainsail trim (near right) is ruined by excessive mainsheet tension (centre). Far right: the outhaul is too slack making the lower third of the sail too full.

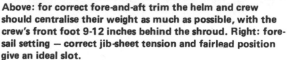

Above: for correct fore-and-aft trim the helm and crew should centralise their weight as much as possible, with the crew's front foot 9-12 inches behind the shroud. Right: fore-sail setting — correct jib-sheet tension and fairlead position give an ideal slot.

Keep the boat upright at all times and make sure your crew is never in your line of vision. If the wind isn't strong enough for him to hike, then get him to lie (rather than sit) on the deck, improving your vision and reducing windage.

Beating in light winds

Conditions. Flat open water, and 0 to 6 knots of wind.

The rig. The vital thing in light winds is to keep the air flowing around the sails. If they are too full the wind won't have enough energy to bend around the excessive camber. Therefore both mainsail and jib must be set as *flat* as possible, with a little more twist than in medium winds. This will mean removing all the chocks from in front of the mast and raking the spreaders aft to induce more bend into the mast, so flattening the mainsail. Tie the top batten with a small amount of tension so as to keep the head of the sail flat, and pull the foot out to the black band. Use 300 to 350 lb of rig tension and move the jib fairleads aft to flatten and open up the leech.

Boat trim. The boat must be kept upright at all times and a slight heel to windward is desirable in winds of 2 to 6 knots. This is effective in that it slightly reduces wetted surface area and, at the same time, keeps the forces mentioned on page 8 working for you. Again, get your crew to trapeze as early as possible; this will mean your sitting on the inside of the side tank and the crew trapezing very high. In winds under 2 knots a slight heel to leeward will pay by reducing wetted surface area, increasing weather helm and 'feel', and helping to keep the sails set. The helm and the crew should be positioned as far forward as possible with the crew against the shroud, so keeping the stern out of the water. Never let your crew sit to leeward of the centreboard case; instead you must sit further in, so keeping your weights closer together.

Centreboard. Angle the centreboard forwards as in medium winds to create weather helm.

Mainsheet, traveller and vang. Pull the traveller up to the windward side so that you can set the mainsail with the boom on the centreline. Cleat the traveller and play the mainsheet, making sure the vang is slack.

Tiller and rudder. If the wind is under 4 knots (non-

In light air it is essential to keep the crew's body out of the slot. The weight of the helm and crew should be together and right forwards (top right). Above: here the helmsman is too far aft, the crew is blocking the slot and the boat is heeling too far. Right: if the wind drops so light that the sails won't fill, the boat needs to be heeled slightly. Come in off the side deck while the crew moves to leeward keeping as low as possible.

trapezing) angle the rudder back 10° to increase feel and weather helm. Hold your tiller lightly by your side and adjust to wind changes with positive but smooth movements.

Cunningham. Fully released.

Steering. Steer as close to the wind as possible, but make sure you don't stop the boat by going too close — in light winds, speed will take a long time to build back again.

Gusts and lulls. As a gust hits, you and your crew should move outboard as in medium winds, tighten the jib sheet to compensate and pull the mainsail in with the mainsheet. Don't adjust the traveller and don't cleat the mainsheet, as in these airs you can feel the wind through the sails' 'pull'. Set the mainsail so that the top streamer is just beginning to break. If the wind drops very light, pull the traveller further to windward and ease the sheet to create more twist.

Concentration. Concentrate on keeping your movements around the boat down to a minimum. Any disturbance will shake the rig and slow you down. Pay more attention to the strength of wind rather

than its direction. Get your crew to be on a constant look-out for more wind and always sail in the direction from where the new wind or more wind is likely to come, even if this means sailing through the windshifts.

Going slowly. The most common cause of bad speed in light airs is incorrect sail shape. Remember, keep the sails as flat as possible.

Non-trapeze boats. All the same principles apply except that when the wind increases you should be the first to hike, leaving your crew either in the boat or lying across the deck.

Rig settings for light-wind beating. Opposite: taking out the mast chocks and angling the spreaders aft gives pre-bend, flattening the sail. The cunningham is right off. Pulling the traveller to weather allows the boom to lie centrally without much mainsheet tension – so the leech is open. Above: the mast is too straight and the leech is closed; therefore the main is stalled and speed will be poor.

Beating in heavy winds

Conditions. Flat open water, and 16 to 35 knots of wind.

The rig. In these winds the rig must be adjusted both to prevent the boat being overpowered and to keep her in balance.

To achieve maximum speed over the water the boat must accelerate of its own accord without much help from you. Adjust your mast bend so that the mainsail sets as flat as possible whilst still maintaining a tight leech. This will mean setting the mast reasonably straight using mast chocks and raking the spreaders further forward to compensate for the extra force introduced by the vang. Rake the mast 3 to 4 inches further aft (measuring from tip of mast to top of transom). This will keep the boat in balance — the adjustment is necessary because your boom will be sheeted further outboard in strong winds. Rig tension should be increased to 350 to 400 lb. Move the jib fairleads aft and pull the mainsail foot out to the black band.

Boat trim. Sail the boat absolutely upright with the crew trapezing low enough to be just skimming the water. You should be hiked out as far as possible but in a comfortable enough position to play the main-sheet and steer the boat efficiently. Keep your weights together, with the crew's front foot 18 to 24 inches behind the shroud.

Centreboard. Rake the board aft 10°. This will help you to keep the boat upright and stop her luffing in the gusts.

Mainsheet, traveller and vang. Set the traveller in the centre of the boat and use vang tension to control the twist in the sail. As the top streamer will be flowing all the time pull the vang progressively harder until you are no longer overpowered. If the mast isn't stiff enough, horizontal creases will appear out of the luff behind the mast before you have sufficient leech tension. If this happens use more chocks or rake the spreaders further forward.

Tiller and rudder. The rudder must be vertical, if not the helm will become heavy and weather helm increase. Hold the tiller in front of you and be very positive about the direction you want the boat to go.

Cunningham. Pull on enough tension to remove the creases forming behind the mast. If you are still over-powered pull on more as this will bend the top of the mast and open the top third of the mainsail.

Left: strong-wind beating. The traveller has been set correctly in the centre allowing the boom to fall off over the quarter. There is too much heel — the crew is lifted too high.

Steering. In these winds, speed is more important than pointing high. Always keep the boat going fast; if you do slow down pressure on the sails increases and you become overpowered and end up throwing away valuable energy by easing sheets.

Gusts and lulls. As a gust hits, ease both sheets together while keeping the boat going straight. When the boat has reached its new speed pull the sails back in and head up closer to the wind. A 'swooping' course should be steered through the gusts and lulls.

Concentration. Concentrate on keeping the boat level and going fast, adjusting the sails constantly to the changes in wind speed. Make sure you get into the right shift sequence as extra tacks will cost you three or four boat lengths.

Going slowly. Make sure you have the correct rig tension as a sagging jib luff closes the slot and makes the entry of the sail too full. Adjust the mainsheet constantly in gusty conditions, as a heel to leeward will reduce speed dramatically.

Non-trapeze boats. Because there is not the same leverage without a trapeze, 'powering' the boat along will not pay unless you have a heavy all-up crew weight. Therefore keep the jib sheeted in tight and stay hard on the wind, playing the mainsheet in the gusts and lulls. Don't raise the centreboard unless the consitions are severe as it will prevent you from pointing (with the jib sheeted in tight the bow will tend to be blown away from the wind).

2 Beating through waves

Beating through waves in medium winds

Conditions. Six-foot high waves, 30 feet between crests, and 6 to 15 knots of wind.

The rig. In these conditions maximum power is required from the rig. Chock the mast at deck level and adjust the spreader angle to induce 2 inches of pre-bend into the mast, measuring from the tip of the gooseneck. Ease the outhaul 1 inch and move the jib fairleads 2 inches further forward than the setting for flat water. Keep the rig tension at 350 lb.

Boat trim. Helm and crew should be as close together as possible with the crew's forward foot 6 inches further aft than in flat water. Sail the boat level. Both the helm and crew should move far enough aft going down the waves to stop the bow burying in the trough, and then forward as they begin rising up the next wave to help the boat over the new crest and on down the next wave. Because there is less wind in the troughs than on the crests, your crew will have to move inboard by bending his knees to compensate for the reduction in power. In extreme sea conditions you will also have to come in from a hiked position to one of sitting on the deck. Once the boat begins to climb up the new wave both of you should move back outboard and at the same time forward, to keep the boat level.

Mainsheet, traveller and vang. Set the vang so that the mainsheet is controlling the leech tension but the vang takes the load the moment you ease the mainsheet. Cleat the traveller, setting the boom 2 inches down to leeward of the centreline at the stern. Play the sheet constantly, easing it out as you go down a wave and pulling it back in as you go up.

Steering. A 'swooping' course through the waves must be steered to produce maximum speed in these conditions. To achieve this you must steer closer to the wind as the boat climbs the wave (windward tell-tale just lifting) and, on reaching the top, bear away for the descent. As you begin the climb to the top, boat speed decreases and pressure on the sails increases as you approach the crest. You must, therefore, steer closer to the wind to counteract this extra force while, at the same time, hiking and trapezing as effectively as possible. As you reach the top, bear away, ease sheets (1 to 2 inches on the jib and enough mainsheet to keep the boat level) and accelerate down the wave into the next trough. As you reach the bottom, pull the sheets back in and head up into the next wave once more (see pages 22-3).

Concentration. Concentrate at all times on keeping the boat moving fast, because if you take a wave badly you will lose several boat lengths. It is better to steer around a bad wave and give away distance to leeward rather than stop the boat by slamming into it. As you weave around the waves keep a constant check on your compass as this is your only way of detecting a shift in these conditions.

Beating through waves in heavy winds

Conditions. Six to 10 foot waves, 30 to 35 feet between crests, and 15 to 28 knots of wind.

The rig. This should be set up as for flat water except that the jib should be set 1 inch further forward so that when the sail is eased going down the waves the top doesn't open out so far that it ceases to do any work.

Boat trim. Both helm and crew should move further aft with the crew's back foot level with the traveller. Again both should move forward and back, going up and down the waves, with the boat kept absolutely level.

Centreboard. Lift the centreboard by 2 inches to reduce weather helm in the gusts.

Steering. Steer the same course as in medium winds with both sheets eased out more. If you are still overpowered move the jib fairleads progressively back until you are in control. Keep the boat moving at maximum speed and don't try to steer too close to

the wind as this will only push you sideways (to leeward).

Beating through waves in light winds

Conditions. Three to 6 foot waves, 25 to 30 feet between crests, and 0 to 6 knots of wind.

The rig. Settings should be the same as in flat water except move the jib fairleads 1 inch further forward and ease the sheet 1 inch to give a slightly fuller and more powerful sail.

Boat trim. Helmsman and crew should position themselves as close together as possible with the crew's forward foot 6 inches behind the shroud going up the waves, and moving aft going down into the troughs. Don't ease the traveller when going down the waves as you will be throwing energy away. Instead both

you and your crew should be alert and ready to hike or trapeze to keep the boat level as she accelerates down each wave.

Mainsheet, traveller and vang. These controls should be set in the same way as for flat water (page 14).

Steering. Steer the same 'swooping' course as in medium winds, keeping the boat moving at all times.

Beating through a chop

Conditions. Three foot waves, 15 feet between crests.

The rig. Set the boat up to produce maximum power from the rig as described earlier. Move the jib fairleads 2 inches further forward than in flat water and ease the sheet 1 inch to produce a more powerful shape. Keep the rig tension on 350 lb.

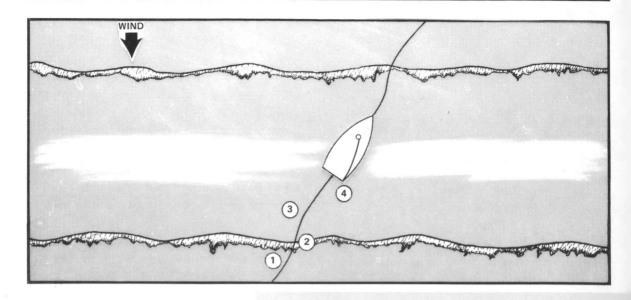

2

1

4

3

1 As the boat's bow goes up the wave, move your weight
   back and begin to luff, while the crew also steps back.
2 On the crest of the wave bear away, and both move your
   weight forward.
3 Ease sheets to accelerate down the back of the wave with
   your crew trapezing flat out.
4 Head up again in the trough and sheet in both sails ready
   for the next wave.

Boat trim. These are certainly the most difficult conditions to sail in and a great deal of practice is required to perfect your technique. Helmsman and crew should position themselves as close together as possible with the crew's back foot level with the traveller. If a really big wave is approaching the crew must step further aft, stepping forward again if the waves ahead become smaller. Sail the boat level, and in smaller seas a heel to windward will pay.

Centreboard. The centreboard should be all the way down unless you are overpowered, in which case raise it 2 inches.

Mainsheet, traveller and vang. Set the mainsail with the mainsheet controlling leech tension and cleat the vang so that it comes into effect for the tacks only. Play the traveller in the gusts, pulling it up as you head into each wave and easing it back down as you bear away. If you do 'take' a wave badly and slow down, ease the mainsheet to create more twist in the sail and only pull it back in when the boat is up to full speed.

Steering. The technique for sailing through a chop is very similar to sailing in a swell; the major difference is the speed at which your rudder operates. As you hit each crest your boat's bow must be turning into the wave, striking it as square on as possible. This is because the waves will be coming down towards you in the same direction as the wind and will, consequently, be slamming into your weather side. By presenting your boat's 'sharp point' to the wave you reduce resistance. As soon as you have headed into the wave and got your bow through it bear away to gather speed ready for the next one. Steering a zig-zag course like this will, if done properly, result in a faster course over the ground than simply steering straight and letting each wave slam into the side of the boat.

Below: tacking.

3 Tacking

A tack in itself is a fairly simple operation, but to perfect it requires many hours of practice alone. In anything other than the lightest of winds tacking will always lose you distance, and it is, therefore, vital that your tacks are perfect.

Tacking in medium winds

Conditions. Six to 15 knots of wind.

The approach. Assume you are beating hard on the wind, fully hiked and your crew flat out on the trapeze. First warn your crew that you are considering a tack. He can then raise himself with his trapeze adjusters and generally prepare himself, so making the manoeuvre easier. When you eventually decide to tack shout "Let's go" or words to that effect. Steer the boat into the wind, leaving the mainsheet cleated or holding it with the same amount of·tension. As your crew comes in off his trapeze he should sheet the jib in harder, sit down on the deck, unhook, and begin to step over the centreboard case towards the other side. You should by then be pushing the boat further into the wind. As you reach 'head to wind' both of you should cross the boat as quickly and smoothly as possible. Your crew should back the jib enough to help the boat around so that you can avoid excessive rudder movement. Once on the new tack your crew should pull the jib in gradually but not completely with one hand, and go straight out on the trapeze

holding the handle with his other hand. When he is out over the side he should hook on and pull the jib into its marked position. At the same time you will have crossed the boat, eased enough mainsheet to keep the boat in balance and be fully hiked before pulling the sheet back in when the boat is back up to full speed and level.

Changing hands on tiller and mainsheet. Assume you are on starboard tack, your tiller in your left hand and the mainsheet in your right. Push the tiller across the boat and keep hold of sheet and tiller with the same hands. Cross the boat while turning, facing forwards, still with sheet and tiller in the same hands. When you reach the other side, sit down; your tiller will still be in your left hand behind your back, and your mainsheet in your right. Slide your right hand along the sheet until you are holding both sheet and tiller in that hand. Then take your left hand from behind your back and grasp the sheet.

Coming out of the tack. Once you have gone through the wind it is advantageous to steer an 'S' course until speed is built back up. To do this keep the boat 10° off the wind after the tack and head slowly back into the wind once you have reached maximum speed. Don't, however, bear away further than this or you will lose too much distance to leeward.

Tacking in waves

Tacking in waves is all about picking your moment to turn. If, for instance, you tack as you hit a wave you will probably end up going backwards and lose many boat lengths. Time your tack so that you are putting the tiller across just as you start going down the

wave. By doing this you can complete your tack before you reach the next wave.

Tacking in light winds

In the lightest of winds, say under 3 knots, it is possible in most boats to gain distance when tacking. You must remember, however, that you are only allowed by the rules to tack for a reason other than propulsion, and this cuts your tacks down to about one per minute. If you do more than this you run the risk of being disqualified by a jury or fellow competitor.

Conditions. Zero to 6 knots of wind.

How to roll tack. Assume you are on starboard tack. Prepare yourself and your crew as mentioned earlier, then bear away 5° from the wind to gather more speed. Working together, heel the boat to leeward and luff at the same time. When you are back hard on the wind, call "tack". Your crew should then join you on the weather side, rolling the boat over to weather while you, at the same time, put the tiller across. Do not cross the boat until you are past head to wind but heel the boat over to weather as far as possible without taking water over the side. As soon as the boat has turned halfway between head to wind and the new closehauled course, both of you should cross the boat as quickly as possible, and hike out together on the new side deck, bringing the boat over to

Top: note that the tiller extension and sheet stay in the same hands until the tack is complete. Only then do you grab the tiller extension with the right hand (still holding the sheet) and finally transfer the sheet to the left hand. Opposite: the ability to tack efficiently is vital when trying to clear your wind after the start.

weather on the port tack. At the midpoint of the tack (as the sail flaps) ease the mainsheet and then sheet it back in once on the new tack. Tacking in this way has the effect of 'wafting' the whole rig through as large an arc as possible, forcing air past the sails and driving you forward.

Tacking in heavy winds

Conditions. Sixteen to 28 knots of wind.

Technique. Assume you are on starboard tack. Tell your crew that you wish to tack and will be doing so on the next suitable wave. You can then wait and look for the smallest wave. As the boat reaches the crest of the wave before the one you have picked, call your crew; he can then come in off the trapeze and be ready to tack. Point the boat closer to the wind as he comes in and uncleat both main and jib sheets. As the boat begins to accelerate down your chosen wave put the helm over and cross the boat. As soon as you are on the new tack your crew must be out on his trapeze with you in complete control before you reach the top of the next wave.

4 The weather mark

Rounding the weather mark onto a reach

Before approaching the mark, several points must be clear in your mind so that when your rounding takes place you know exactly what must be done. Firstly, check your compass bearing so you can determine if the reach is going to be close or broad. If the wind is too light for trapezing approach the mark on starboard so that your crew can set the spinnaker pole before you reach the mark, making for a faster spinnaker set. If the wind is stronger it can pay to pass the tiller to your crew and then go forward yourself to set the pole. This manoeuvre depends largely on your position relative to other boats.

Starboard tack approach. Usually it pays to approach the mark on starboard so that you can set the pole as mentioned above and also so that you have right of way over port-tack boats going into the mark. If you have worked out that the wind has backed (making the reach very close) it will pay you to overstand, providing you are not in the first ten coming in to the mark. This is because you can then come into the mark at top speed and stay up to weather of other boats once rounded. Having done this your options are open once you get further down the reach – you can either go high and hoist the spinnaker later or you can bear away and aim straight for the mark. In either case, because the reach is close, you will have gained as your speed will be as good as boats to leeward.

If, however, the wind has veered, then try not to overstand the windward mark as you will probably want to stay down to leeward on the forthcoming reach. To do this you have to be on the inside when rounding the mark so that you can then steer straight without being luffed by boats inside you.

Port tack approach. The port tack into the mark will only pay if:

1   You are well separated from the rest of the fleet and boats reaching down from the weather mark are not going to take your wind as you beat up.

2   The fleet is well spread out and you are confident about finding a gap to tack into between boats approaching on starboard.

The port tack is sometimes effective if boats on starboard are queuing up to go round the mark as they will all be overstanding trying to keep their air clear. But it is a manoeuvre that should be treated with great caution.

The rounding. Assume you have already set the pole on the mast. Before you reach the mark, ease the vang, cunningham and outhaul to their correct reaching positions. As soon as your stern clears the mark bear away onto your chosen course and ease the main and jib sheets. Your crew should clip the spinnaker guy under the reaching hook and uncleat the spinnaker sheet. Now come in from the side deck, stand in the centre of the boat, cleat the mainsheet and hoist the spinnaker, steering with the tiller between your knees. As soon as the spinnaker is up the crew

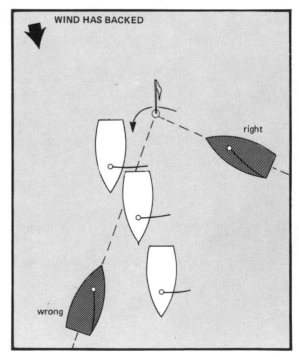

In stronger winds it can pay to set the spinnaker pole yourself on the approach to the windward mark, while the crew takes the tiller.

should cleat the guy with the pole 2 inches off the forestay, and go out on the trapeze taking with him the spinnaker sheet, which you will have handed to him. When he is out on the trapeze with the spinnaker full and pulling, you can adjust the mainsail and jib for maximum drive, raise the centreboard and begin steering your best course to the gybe mark.

Rounding the weather mark onto a run

It is vital to know the true wind direction before you reach the mark as this will tell you which gybe to be on after the rounding. If you are well down the fleet, it will also tell you which tack to be on approaching the mark. For example, if you know the wind has backed you will also know that the fleet will be coming down the run on the starboard gybe and it will, therefore, pay to avoid them by approaching on starboard tack (see diagram). The opposite is true if the wind has veered.

The rounding. Unless the wind has veered more than 10° it will pay to hoist the spinnaker on the starboard gybe and then either stay on starboard or gybe onto port once it is set. By doing this you will be able to carry your way on round the mark and make a faster spinnaker hoist. Set the pole if possible before reaching the mark, ease vang and cunningham as before, and as soon as you have cleared the buoy let the mainsheet go so the mainsail goes out all the way and stops against the shroud; there is no need to waste time cleating the sheet. Hoist the spinnaker as quickly as possible while your crew cleats the guy. Finally pass him the sheet before you sit down on the leeward side.

If the wind has veered more than 10° you have to gybe at the weather mark and will consequently not have set the pole. If this is the case, then ease vang and cunningham before the rounding and gybe onto port as close to the mark as possible, thereby preventing any boats getting inside you and on your wind. As

Rounding the windward mark . . .   **. . . the main and jib sheets are cleated in their reaching positions.**

soon as your gybe is complete and both sheets have
been eased, your crew can put the pole out while you
hoist the spinnaker. As you will have hoisted before
your crew has finished pushing the pole out, it is up
to you to fill the spinnaker. Do this by playing both
sheet and guy while standing up and steering with the
tiller between your knees. When your crew is ready,
hand him the guy first so he can cleat it, and then the
sheet. You can then sit down on the leeward side.

**While the crew cleats the guy I pull the sheet to set the
spinnaker . . .**

The crew sets up the pole while I hoist the spinnaker, steering with my knees.

. . . and then pass the sheet to the crew.

The crew is now fully in charge of the kite while I handle the main and jib sheets.

5 Reaching

Reaching in medium winds

Conditions. Six to 15 knots of wind.

The rig. Good reaching speed is mainly due to correct hull and spinnaker shape. To be competitive your boat must have both; you must also, however, pay attention to the following points.

1   *Mainsail.* If you are using a flat main then everything possible must be done to create more fullness in the sail. Ease the outhaul 3 to 4 inches — most sails are now made with a 'lens foot' which creates more depth in the sail when the outhaul is released and helps downwind speed enormously. Ease both shrouds if possible — this reduces rig tension and straightens the mast creating more fullness in the sail. Ease the cunningham right off.

2   *Jib.* Release the cunningham and move the fairleads forward enough to stop the top of the sail twisting too far off and becoming inefficient.

3   *Spinnaker.* Set the spinnaker pole so that both clews are parallel with the boat. If the pole is too high the weather clew of the sail will be higher than the leeward, and vice versa if the pole is too low. Raise the pole height in stronger winds and lower it in lighter winds to produce maximum efficiency from the design. Make sure your sheet leads are as far back as you can get them in order to keep the leech as open and as far away from the mainsail as possible. Check that your sheets and halyard are non-stretch and of minimum diameter.

The spinnaker guy should be cleated level with the shroud, helping to keep the pole from 'skying' and also reducing the amount of sheet liable to stretch between clew and cleat. When the wind is forward of the beam set the pole 1 inch off the forestay; don't let it touch or you will run the risk of breaking the pole. Never cleat the spinnaker sheet but constantly play it as the wind direction changes, easing the sheet until the luff is just 'breaking'. As speed increases the spinnaker needs to be sheeted in harder due to the apparent wind moving forward. Play the main-sheet in the same way with the luff of the sail just beginning to break.

Boat trim. Providing the class of boat you sail is well balanced, it always pays to keep the boat level. But in classes like the 505 which has a long spinnaker pole the boat develops lee helm, forcing you to sail with 15° of heel to keep it going in a straight line. Helm and crew should be as close together as possible and move forward together on top of any wave to help the boat down and, once surfing, move back aft to stop the bow burying in the trough.

Centreboard. Raise the centreboard enough to stop

Spinnaker settings. Top row: the pole height is set correctly as shown by the clews being level. Below: setting the pole too high (left and centre) closes the leech of the sail choking the slot between spinnaker and mainsail. Right: having the pole too low makes the luff of the spinnaker too round and trimming becomes almost impossible.

Top row: helm and crew reaching positions. In light airs (left) both helm and crew sit as far forward as possible to lift the stern. As the wind increases (right) the crew stays put and the helmsman balances the boat. In medium winds (opposite, left) the crew begins to hike and the helmsman moves to the weather deck; in stronger winds (opposite, right) the crew goes out on the trapeze and if necessary lowers himself (opposite, below) to give more leverage.

the boat slipping sideways; in most cases half the area down would be correct.

Steering. Make sure your rudder is vertical — if it isn't the helm will be heavy and control not 100 per cent.

If there are no other boats around you a straight line course to the mark is usually the best. However, in gusty conditions it pays to luff up in the lulls and bear away in the gusts, keeping boat speed more constant but sailing a greater distance.

It is important always to keep an eye on the wind to weather and ahead, because if you spot a gust coming down towards you it may pay to luff up and get into it early, then bear away back on course with greater speed. If, however, you see that the wind is dropping light it would pay to bear away, so that you can luff up when you hit less wind and keep your speed constant.

If the reach is too close to set your spinnaker, it can pay to luff up 10° above the course to the mark and sail three-quarters of the reach before bearing away back on course and hoisting the spinnaker. By doing this you sail a greater distance but more than make up for it in speed.

Reaching in light winds

Conditions. Zero to 6 knots of wind.

The rig. In the lightest of winds never create too much fullness in the mainsail as it will tend to stall. Ease the outhaul 1 to 2 inches, free the cunningham and ease the vang until there is sufficient twist to make the top streamer just begin to flow. Ease the jib cunningham and move the fairleads 2 inches forward. Lower the spinnaker pole to keep the clews level and the sail pulling properly. If the reach becomes very close, pull the traveller to weather to retain sufficient twist in the sail.

Boat trim. In these conditions both helm and crew should be seated well forward, the crew up against the shroud on the weather side and the helmsman in front of the traveller down to leeward. It is the helmsman's job to balance the boat and in gusts and lulls he should be moving in or outboard, leaving the crew to focus all his attention on setting the spinnaker. If there is a sudden gust, the helmsman should move onto the weather side, positioning himself either on the deck or inboard astride the traveller. Never let your crew go out on the trapeze until you are to weather of the centreline. In marginal trapezing conditions it pays to let your crew stay out on the trapeze while you balance the boat, moving from the side deck to the centreline.

Centreboard. Raise the centreboard enough to stop sideways 'slip' — usually leaving half of the board in the water is correct.

Steering. Be very gentle on the helm, making smooth and small changes in direction. If the wind drops, head up to keep speed on and the spinnaker filling, wait for a good enough gust and then carefully bear away as far as possible without collapsing the spinnaker. It is generally an advantage to steer above your course for the mark if this is the only way to keep your spinnaker filling.

Reaching in heavy winds

Conditions. Sixteen to 35 knots of wind.

The rig. If you find yourself overpowered and unable to lay the mark, then a reduction in power is required. You have the following controls to adjust.

1 The outhaul should be pulled out to the black band to flatten the lower third of the sail.

2 Pull the cunningham down as hard as you can; this 'drags' the fullness in the sail forwards, opens up the leech and bends the mast, flattening the sail.

3 Ease the vang progressively until the mainsail is twisted with the top completely open, spilling air out of its upper half. Easing the vang is your only way of spilling the wind out of the mainsail as the spinnaker sheet prevents the boom from moving further outboard than the line between fairlead and clew.

Never oversheet the jib, and in extreme conditions ease it out until the front half of the sail is lifting, thereby dumping more power. Always keep the spinnaker pole 2 inches off the forestay so that the leech of the spinnaker doesn't 'hook' air back into the mainsail (in the diagram below the dotted line shows a poor spinnaker setting).

If you are unable to lay the mark and can foresee no change in the wind's strength or direction, it will pay you to drop the spinnaker and head straight for the mark under mainsail and jib alone.

Boat trim. Position yourselves as close together as possible with your crew's feet either side of the traveller. As you surf down a wave you will both have to move aft to stop the bow burying into the trough. Do not, however, move aft too far or you will dig the stern in the water and raise the bow too far out, creating more windage. Sail the boat level and make sure your crew is as low on his trapeze adjusters as possible. He should be just skimming the wave tops with neither his legs nor his back bent. To do this he will have to play the sheet with one hand — it is not possible to use both hands because the trapeze wire is in the way. You should be hiking as far out as you can get, lying flat so that you don't drag your body through the waves.

Centreboard. Raise the centreboard until you can

Opposite: Fireballs battling strong winds on the reach.

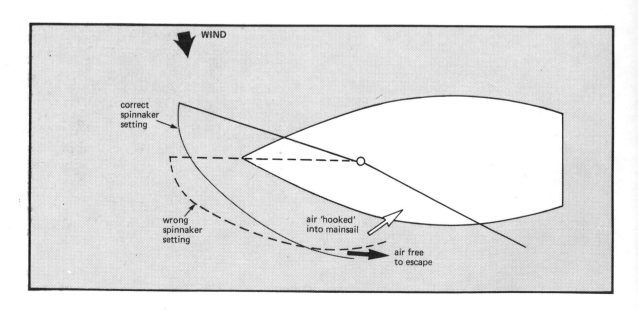

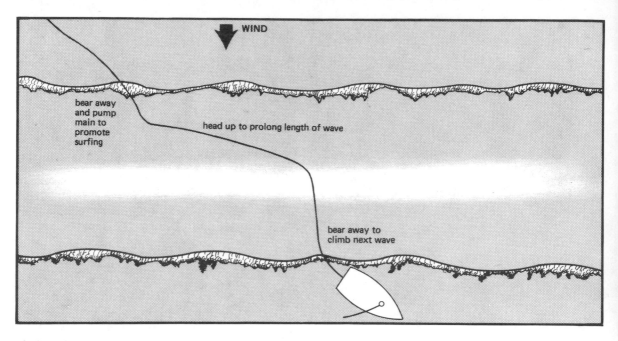

WIND

bear away
and pump
main to
promote
surfing

head up to prolong length of wave

bear away to
climb next wave

feel the boat just begin to slide to leeward: one-third of its area is usually sufficient.

Steering. Luff up in the lulls and bear away in the gusts. In waves you must always be looking ahead for a suitable wave to surf down. As the waves will normally be running across your course you must bear away onto each one to promote surfing; once you are surfing, head up, thereby prolonging the effective length of the wave by steering diagonally along it (see diagram above).

Once you reach the trough again head up to keep your bow out of the back of the next wave, and then sail over this wave and bear away down its face. As you surf down the face, your speed will increase dramatically and you will have to sheet in rapidly due to the apparent wind moving forward.

6 The gybe mark

It is the exit from the gybe mark rather than the approach that is all-important. Always aim to be on the inside of any group of boats and plan your approach down the reach with that in mind. If you do have to give water to another boat you may lose more than one place as other boats can slip in between you and the mark. If another boat does have an overlap, always point the boat directly at the mark and then luff at the last moment before reaching the two boat-lengths circle. This will usually enable you to accelerate away, breaking the overlap. If you are trying to establish an overlap, stay four to five lengths down to leeward of the opposition and reach up to the buoy at the last moment, thereby coming in to the mark at greater speed. But don't luff too soon or you will end up in their windshadow.

Gybing in medium winds

Preparation before you reach the gybe mark is all-important. You must go through the following procedure, whatever your position relative to other boats.

Approximately ten lengths before the mark, cleat the spinnaker guy on the side tank. Then cleat the weather jib sheet, pulling 6 to 9 inches of the jib's clew to weather. Cleat the mainsail in its correct position for the next reach.

When you are two lengths from the mark, uncleat the old jib sheet so the sail is set for the next reach; tell your crew to come in off the trapeze and free off the spinnaker guy from the reaching hook. As you bear away into the gybe your crew should let go of the sheet, pick up the guy which is still cleated on the side tank, and as the boat gybes pull the guy across the boat with him which, in turn, pulls the spinnaker around the forestay and onto the new gybe. This also prevents the spinnaker blowing between the mast and forestay.

As soon as the boat is balanced the crew should immediately take the pole (which is still on the old gybe) off the mast, clip it onto the new guy, push it out and forward, and snap the other end onto the mast. As he is doing this you will have gybed the mainsail by taking hold of the mainsheet directly from the boom, crossed the boat, settled on the new gybe, and (if necessary) adjusted the main and jib sheet. As soon as the sheets are correctly trimmed, pull the guy to its mark and cleat it on the side deck. Then pick up the spinnaker sheet and pass it to your crew who will, by then, have put the guy under the reaching hook, cleated it and hooked on to his trapeze ready to step out once he has filled the spinnaker.

Steering. Always, if possible, approach the mark from above the straight line course. This enables you to bear away onto a broad reach as you approach the last ten lengths of the leg, thereby enabling your crew to come in off the trapeze to unhook himself and the spinnaker guy, ready for the gybe. It also means that you can do a smoother and more controlled gybe as your boat will be gybing through a smaller angle. In some cases it is possible to complete your gybe *before* you reach the mark by sailing the last few lengths on a run, and gybing while still running. This is particularly effective when the second reach is very close, in that it enables you to steer immediately for the next mark, without giving away distance to leeward while completing the gybe.

Vang and centreboard. As you approach the mark, make sure your vang is well eased, as this raises the boom, reducing the chances of it hitting the water immediately after gybing. It also reduces pressure on the mainsail due to the wind escaping out of the top. Make sure the centreboard is approximately halfway down as too much will cause the boat to 'trip over' itself, and too little will make the boat unstable.

Timing. Always gybe when the boat is going at full speed as this is when there is the least pressure on the sails. If you are accelerating or slowing down, the pressure on the sails is obviously greater. You can experience this when surfing down steep waves — on occasions your boom will 'drift' towards the centreline of the boat on its own accord, due to the boat going

Rounding the gybe mark. The crew comes in off the trapeze, uncleats the guy from the reaching hook and pulls the jib round. The helm begins to pull the boom over as the crew begins to pull the guy around to windward.

The crew takes the pole off the mast and clips it on to the new guy before pushing the pole out and clipping the end on to the mast.

The crew puts the new guy under the reaching hook. Reverse
the tiller as the boom comes over.

The crew pulls the guy around to its mark while the helmsman pulls in the spinaker sheet. The helmsman passes the
sheet to the crew while the crew hooks on the trapeze.

faster than the wind. Therefore whenever possible, gybe going down a wave, never in a trough or riding up a wave.

Once you have begun to gybe, never change your mind as this will nearly always end in a capsize. Begin your turn by slowly bearing away until you are running dead downwind. Once you have reached this point, pull the tiller a little harder, give a good pull on the mainsheet to bring the boom over, and then cross the boat. Your mainsheet is cleated so you only have to worry about your tiller. As soon as the boom has crossed the centreline, correct your turning moment with a sharp pull the other way on the tiller. This effectively 'kills' the boat's turning momentum and gets you on a straight course for the mark.

Gybing in light winds

When gybing in light winds it is most important to sail the shortest possible course around the mark without either slowing the boat or collapsing the spinnaker. To do this a great deal of coordination is required between helmsman and crew. Your crew will not be trapezing and should be playing both sheet and guy without using any cleats. With two lengths to go to the mark you should take the spinnaker sheet and guy from him, stand in the middle of the boat and steer with the tiller between your knees leaving your hands free to trim the spinnaker. It is the crew's job to pull the boom across and balance the boat. Remember that in light winds the speed of the whole operation is irrelevant and the speed and direction of the boat all-important. The crew should, therefore, be careful not to collapse the spinnaker when switching the pole over from one gybe to the other.

Steering. Approaching the mark, aim to be one length to weather of it with two lengths to go. This enables you to bear away slowly, while at the same time 'squaring' the pole around without collapsing the spinnaker. Any boats behind cannot overtake you immediately after the gybe by doing a tighter turn or by heading up above you after the gybe, because they will slow down in doing this. So you can sail this course regardless of other competitors.

Vang and centreboard. Leave the centreboard half-

Left: during a run-to-run gybe steer with your knees, cleat the main and play the spinnaker sheet and guy while the crew sets the pole. Opposite: whenever possible gybe going down a wave to reduce the pressure on the sail.

way down to stop the boat rolling after the gybe. Cleat the mainsheet and vang in their positions for the next reach.

Gybing in heavy winds

If the wind is less than 28 knots a good gybe with a spinnaker is possible. In winds over 28 knots it is better simply to get around the mark, regardless of speed, and stay upright!

As mentioned previously, the only time to gybe is when going at maximum speed and, in strong winds, if you do try to gybe at any other time you will almost certainly capsize. No matter how good a helmsman you are, 28 knots of wind hitting a boat going, say, 3 knots, will strike with tremendous force. Therefore get your boat speed as near to the wind speed as possible.

Steering. You must approach the mark from well to windward so that your crew can come in off the trapeze to unhook himself and the spinnaker guy. By coming into the mark on a run you can pick your moment and wave to gybe on, and once gybed can make a close rounding of the mark. Any boats that come in directly from the previous mark will not be able to pick their moment and will either capsize at the mark or sail straight past it, waiting for a suitable moment to gybe. They will, consequently, lose distance to leeward on the second reach and on an Olympic course will never 'fetch' the leeward mark with their spinnaker flying. They will also be on the outside at the leeward mark and be forced to give water to other boats.

Vang and sheets. Ease the vang until the mainsail is twisted well off. Before coming into the gybe make sure that your main will not be oversheeted for the next reach and, in extreme conditions, leave the mainsheet uncleated so that you can either pull or ease it immediately after the gybe to balance the boat. Do the same with the jib, making sure it is well eased for the next reach.

7 The leeward mark

As you approach the leeward mark you must be aware of any changes in wind direction as they can help you in deciding which way you go up the next beat. If, for example, the reach has gradually become broader as you approach the mark, there may well be a wind bend and if so, it would pay you to hold on the port tack rather than tacking away after you have rounded the mark (as in the diagram).

In all cases plan your strategy for the beat before you round the mark. Providing no other boats are taking your wind or trying to gain an overlap on you, the best approach to the mark is to stay half a length to leeward of the rhumb line so that when you drop the spinnaker you can come into the buoy reaching at full speed. If you go high on the reach you will end up running down to the mark with little speed and having to make a tight turn as you round.

Rounding with a spinnaker chute

Approaching the mark with ten lengths to go, put your centreboard down ready for the beat, then pull cunningham, vang and outhaul to their marks. With your crew still on the trapeze, move into the centre of the boat, steer with your knees, uncleat the halyard and pull the spinnaker into the chute. Your crew should balance the boat and ease both guy and sheet before coming in off the trapeze to take the pole down. If you are trying to gain an overlap on another boat it will pay to leave your spinnaker flying longer, dropping it at the last moment and taking the pole down once on the beat. The best way to do this is to pass the tiller to your crew and then go forward and take the pole down.

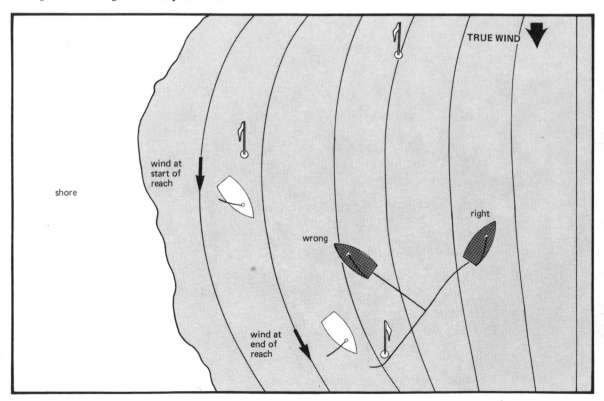

Rounding the leeward mark. Top row: the helmsman lowers the centreboard, and tightens the outhaul. The crew takes down the spinnaker pole. Centre: The helmsman uncleats the spinnaker halyard, steering with his knees, while the spinnaker is pulled down. Below: the spinnaker should be stowed and the vang and cunningham set up for the beat in time to allow you to concentrate on a good rounding.

Rounding without a spinnaker chute

Arrange your course so that you can bear away when your crew needs to come in off the trapeze. Essentially this means approaching the mark one boat length higher than with a spinnaker chute. With fifteen lengths to go, put the centreboard down and pull in vang, cunningham and outhaul. With ten lengths to go, take the spinnaker sheet from your crew and tell him to come in off the trapeze and take the spinnaker down. As he takes the pole off the mast you can keep the spinnaker pulling as you still have a hold of the sheet. He then gathers in the foot of the sail and you uncleat the halyard, easing it off along with the sheet and making sure you don't drop the sail faster than he can stow it in its bag. With the sail stowed away the crew can then go back out on his trapeze and you can sheet in and round the mark. Then check your controls and pull in any loose sheets trailing in the water.

8 Running

Running in medium winds

You can gain or lose more distance on the run than on any other leg of the course. It is, therefore, important to know how to achieve good boat speed and how to make use of any changes in the wind.

Conditions. Six to 15 knots of wind.

The rig. Ease both shrouds off to bring the mast more upright in the boat. This increases the effective sail area by adding height to the rig. The balance of the boat will not change whatever the mast rake, so it is obviously an advantage to keep the mast upright. Ease the vang enough to let the mainsail set with a small degree of twist. A good way to judge this is to line up the last 9 inches of the top batten with the boom, keeping the two parallel. If you are sailing with the wind dead astern, pull the outhaul out to its black band to increase projected sail area. Raise the centreboard as far as possible without making the boat unstable but never raise it completely as the slot gaskets will be less effective, resulting in extra turbulence inside the centreboard case.

Cleat the jib in its position for broad reaching so that if the wind shifts abeam the jib will be set to its correct trim.

Adjust the spinnaker pole height, keeping both clews level and, normally, never bring the pole aft of a continuation line of the boom. Always remember to fly the spinnaker a good distance away from the jib luff, never pulling the pole back so far as to choke the sail, thus preventing air flowing out of its base. Also never let the pole go too far forward because you would lose projected area by bringing the clews too close together. Ease the cunningham on both main and jib.

The spinnaker pole should be just forward of a line through the boom (top right). Pulling it too far back (left) creates a shelf at the foot of the sail which prevents the air from escaping; but if the pole is too far forward (below) you lose projected area.

Opposite: mainsail twist on the run. The correct setting is shown far left, with the last few inches of the top batten in line with the boom. Too much twist (left, top) results in loss of power in the top of the sail and causes the boat to roll to weather. Too little twist (left, below) stalls the top of the sail. This page: spinnaker pole height. The clews should be level (right). Having the pole too low (top) prevents air flowing across the spinnaker while having it too high (above) closes the leech and makes the spinnaker unstable and difficult to trim.

On the run, loosen the leeward shroud so that the boom can be squared off (for maximum projected area).

Boat trim. Going down the run in a spinnaker boat the helmsman should always sit to leeward and the crew to windward. This enables the crew to concentrate his full attention on trimming the spinnaker, leaving the helmsman to balance the boat, look out for waves to surf down, check the wind direction and other competitors' positions. In non-planing conditions the crew should be right up against the shroud with the helmsman forward of the traveller, lifting the stern out of the water and reducing wetted surface area. The crew should be seated on the deck with his feet hooked under the toe-straps so that he can lean in or out in any gusts or lulls he detects through the pull of the spinnaker. He should also play both sheet and guy continuously, with the guy running directly from the clew of the sail to his hand. By doing this he can make rapid adjustments to the trim of the sail as the wind changes or the helmsman alters course. The helmsman should sit on the leeward side deck holding the tiller in one hand and the mainsheet

directly from the boom in the other. He can then feel any extra wind hitting the sail which would otherwise be undetected if the sheet had to run through a normal four-to-one purchase system.

Steering. In non-planing conditions it is difficult to know your downwind tacking angle. In a Finn dinghy, for example, you can let the boom out at right angles to the boat and can, therefore, steer dead downwind. In other classes it pays to sail a series of broad reaches, tacking downwind. The angle you choose depends on speed against distance and works in the same way as when beating, in that for every degree you head up you must go significantly faster to make up for the extra distance sailed. The technique is first to reach up closer to the wind, building up more speed and moving the apparent wind forwards. Then, as speed is achieved, bear away again still keeping speed on, which in turn leaves the apparent wind effectively on your stern quarter instead of dead astern. In gusts, again head up as the wind drops and bear away as it picks up.

Steer through the waves by reaching up to gain speed to overtake the next wave in front. As soon as the boat begins to surf bear away down the wave and head back towards the mark. Sail by the lee so as to move diagonally along the wave and ride it as long as possible. Just before you hit the trough head up again and, with your crew, move aft to lift the bow over the next wave and on down its face.

Running in light winds

Conditions. Zero to 6 knots of wind.

The rig. Set this up as for medium winds, but make sure your spinnaker sheets are of minimum diameter.

Boat trim. Both helm and crew should sit right up against the shrouds to lift the transom and reduce wetted surface area.

Sail the boat with a slight heel to windward as this helps to keep the spinnaker filling (providing you are dead downwind with the majority of the sail over on the weather side). Hold the boom out with your hand to stop it swinging into the centre of the boat and don't worry if the sail does not appear to be filling. If you do heel the boat to leeward you will get a better-looking mainsail by making it set under its own weight; it will not, however, be any faster as it is still projected area that is required on a run. The important factor is keeping the spinnaker filled.

Above: On a light-weather run you must keep the spinnaker pulling but without sailing too much extra distance. When the spinnaker begins to collapse, head up (which brings the apparent wind forwards) to fill the spinnaker; once you have regained speed bear away back on course.

Steering. Bear away on any small gust that you get and head back up in the lulls. Always steer to keep the spinnaker filling — this will mean constantly altering course, heading up as you see the sail begin to collapse and back down as boat speed improves. A good understanding with your crew is necessary and he must tell you when he feels you can bear away a little and still keep the spinnaker filling, or should head up because it is beginning to collapse. In order to keep speed up in these conditions you may find you have to steer well above the rhumb line. Obviously, if you have to sail twice the distance to the leeward mark to keep the spinnaker filling, you know you must go at least twice as fast and in the lightest of airs this is hard to achieve. It is usually advantageous to sail a course somewhere in between, accepting that your spinnaker will not be filling for some of the time.

Running in heavy winds

Conditions. Sixteen to 35 knots of wind.

The rig. Always keep a check on the twist in your mainsail as too much vang will slow you down and too little will make the boat unstable. Line up the top batten with the boom as in medium winds. Only ease the shrouds off in winds under 20 knots as in stronger winds the mast will need the support.

Boat trim. If the wind is strong but under 28 knots the helmsman should sit on the leeward side deck behind the traveller. The crew is to weather but further aft than in medium conditions. Use your weight in waves: if you are sailing down long rollers, for example, you should sit with your legs either side of the traveller and slide your weight forward to help the boat down the face, then back again before you get to the trough. If the wind is over 28 knots you must still fly the spinnaker but with the helmsman

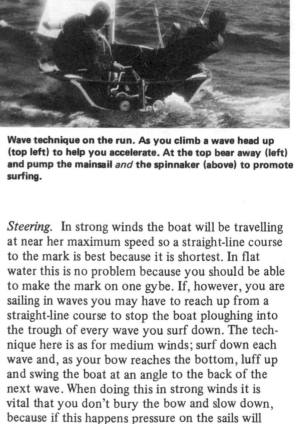

Wave technique on the run. As you climb a wave head up (top left) to help you accelerate. At the top bear away (left) and pump the mainsail *and* the spinnaker (above) to promote surfing.

to weather and the crew to leeward. The crew should cleat the spinnaker guy and play the sheet as he would a jib in a non-spinnaker boat — by doing this he is free to move around and balance the boat. Meanwhile the helmsman concentrates on steering the boat through the waves and, being to weather, is in a better position to see dangerous waves and gusts approaching.

Centreboard. Leave half the centreboard down — any less may result in the boat rolling and becoming unstable.

Steering. In strong winds the boat will be travelling at near her maximum speed so a straight-line course to the mark is best because it is shortest. In flat water this is no problem because you should be able to make the mark on one gybe. If, however, you are sailing in waves you may have to reach up from a straight-line course to stop the boat ploughing into the trough of every wave you surf down. The technique here is as for medium winds; surf down each wave and, as your bow reaches the bottom, luff up and swing the boat at an angle to the back of the next wave. When doing this in strong winds it is vital that you don't bury the bow and slow down, because if this happens pressure on the sails will increase dramatically and you will run the risk of either capsizing or losing your mast over the front.

Part 2
The race

9 Preparation

Before any regatta begins you must prepare yourself and the boat. On arriving at the venue do not stroll around the dinghy park examining other boats; you will have plenty of time to do this after the regatta, and it may raise doubts in your mind about the quality of your own boat in comparison to later fancy models. Concentrate instead on your own boat and either work on it or stay away from the park. Make sure you have done any major work to your boat before you arrive — last-minute sanding of boards and rudders should be avoided as it will take your mind off more important matters.

If possible, try to arrive one week before the championship to acclimatise and familiarise yourself with the surroundings. Go out and sail three or four hours a day to get used to the wave and wind patterns. You can usually pick up local shifts and tide effects and generally get a better feeling for the course you will compete on. Check out the tide on the course; get hold of a chart of the area and write down times and directions of flow so that you can transfer them to your boat prior to each race.

Unless you are allowed several suits of sails in a series, decide well in advance which ones you are going to have measured, as last-minute decisions will only divert your line of thought away from the race itself. Never choose sails that perform only in certain conditions (conditions seldom remain constant for a full week), but pick the sails that will be good in all conditions.

If possible have back-up sails, identical sails to the ones you are using, and make sure they *are* identical before you arrive at the venue. If you don't have these and tear a sail you are unlikely to perform as well with your second choice, if only for psychological reasons.

Before the race

Arrive at the park three hours before the start, check the weather forecast and go and rig your boat. Make sure all shackles, split pins, etc. are in order, and prepare for launching. Get changed and make another check of the weather forecast. Unless you are convinced the wind will be light always take your weight jacket out in a polythene bag. You can then either soak the weight jacket or leave it dry in the bag. If water bottles are allowed take them out full — if the wind stays light simply dump the water from the bottles before the five-minute gun.

Make sure you know the sailing instructions, and check the notice board for any changes. Be on the water so that you are in the race area with 45 minutes to the start. Remember to take out plenty of fluid and also some chocolate or glucose.

Tides

Unless you are sailing on a small inland water, tides and currents always play a major part in championship strategy.

Before any series begins you must have access to good charts of the area. If you have these you can gain most of the information you need before you even arrive. You can also familiarise yourself with the surrounding land and generally get to know more about the course you are preparing to sail on.

Once you have a chart, make out your own list of water speeds and directions, something like this:

Hours to high water	water speed	direction
6	1.0 knot	020°
5	1.5 knots	035°
4	2.0 knots	040°
3	2.0 knots	045°
2	1.5 knots	050°
1	0.5 knot	050°

You can then stick this to your boat (covering it with see-through plastic) for use in every race. For example, if your start is at 3:00 pm and high water at 6:00 pm you will know that the tide is running in a direction of 045° at 2.0 knots at your start. You can then work out that on your last beat the flow will have moved to 050° and reduced to 0.5 knots in speed. This should give you an advantage over most of your rivals who will only know speed and direction of the tide at the start of the race.

Checking tides on days before the race is also useful, but usually the chart gives the best information however, always look out for local effects when you are sailing close to the shore, and remember that the tide turns first inshore.

Using the tide

Always be careful on the start line when there is a lot of tide. If it is still running with you it will pay to hold back behind the line and come in fast and late whilst other boats are reaching along the line trying to stay behind it.

If the flow is against you beware of being late across the line, and in light airs, providing there is no one-minute or five-minute rule, it invariably pays to stay above the line, dipping back behind it 15 seconds before the gun. This manoeuvre may sound risky, but you are in a position of having greater speed than boats to leeward and, therefore, can pick your spot along the line when you see a gap.

If the tide is along the line it makes the start difficult to judge. For example, if the tide is running right to left and it is a port-end start, make sure you are not too early. Most sailors underestimate the strength of the tide and, with careful calculation, you should always be able to capitalise on a strong tide and make a good start at either end.

On the beat always try to get the flow on your lee bow. Whatever you have read about this theory, believe me, it pays. It is even worth pointing a little high and losing speed if it means your switching the flow from your weather bow to your lee bow.

Forming a race plan

Having left the beach, usually an hour and a half before the start, check for wind shifts or bends on your way to the start line. If it is a beat you can note shifts on the way. If it is a reach or run, steer a straight-line compass course and check which way the wind has been changing relative to your sails. If you think there may be a difference in wind direction at the start line and the first mark you must go and check. If, for example, the wind is on 220° at the start area and 240° at the weather mark, it would certainly pay to put a long port tack in off the start to take advantage of a veered wind bend.

If you cannot detect any wind bends then, on arriving at the start area, begin taking wind readings by either sailing close-hauled on both tacks and dividing your readings by 2, or by simply pointing your boat directly head to wind. Have a piece of white plastic stuck on your boat to write on with a chinagraph pencil and keep a record of the wind direction at five-minute intervals to get a pattern of the wind oscillations, as in the following example.

10:30 am	Wind direction 240°
10:35 am	+ 5°
10:40 am	+10°
10:45 am	+ 5°
10:50 am	0
10:55 am	− 5°
11:00 am	− 10°
11:05 am	− 15°
11:10 am	− 10°

Having checked these oscillations a pattern will emerge and you will get an idea of what the wind is doing — if it is shifting around a mean direction or if it is gradually backing or veering. If it is the former it will pay to tack on the shifts, bearing in mind any tidal effects. If it is the latter and it is gradually veering (shifting clockwise), it would pay to play the shifts but stay over on the starboard side of the course to take advantage of the slowly veering wind. Always keep in mind the weather forecast and, most important, the way the majority of the fleet are going. In any decisions of strategy you must never leave the fleet, even if you are convinced your wind predictions are correct.

10 Starting and finishing

With half an hour to the start continue taking wind bearings and familiarise yourself with the conditions of the day by doing practice beats with other boats. Make sure you have the correct settings for the conditions and do not start making major alterations to your rig unless you have tried them before. Concentrate instead on sailing the boat as quickly as possible with what you know to be about right. Keep checking the wind and don't stray too far from the start line in case the wind drops. If the windward and gybe marks have been laid check that they are in the position the race committee says they are by their magnetic bearing. Work out your compass bearings for the first reach, second reach and run, for example:

Windward mark bears 200°
Gybe mark is therefore 065° (first reach)
Leeward mark is therefore 335° (second reach)
Leeward mark is therefore 020° (run)

Always remember that if you sail longer on starboard tack going up the beat you will sail longer on port down the run, and vice versa. Check also the wind direction in relation to your heading on both tacks (for example: wind direction 200°; starboard tack 155°; port tack 245°). If you then start heading 135° on starboard you will know the wind has backed to 180° leaving the first reach very close and the second reach very broad. It will also mean a long run on the starboard gybe (probably all the way) and anybody who hasn't worked this out may gybe onto port if he can't see the mark and automatically lose places.

As soon as you have finally set your boat up for the conditions and decided what the wind is doing, go back to the start line and sail directly along it checking its compass bearing. Do this by starting off right by the committee boat and pointing straight towards the leeward end buoy. By knowing this bearing and the wind direction you can work out precisely the favoured end of the line.

In the diagram the wind direction is 200° and the line bearing is 120°. This line would be square if its bearing were 110°, so it has a 10° bias to the port end.

Any good race officer would normally set the line with a 5° port-end bias so if he gives you a windward mark bearing of 200° you would expect the line to bear 115°. Again know the wind direction because if it changes so will the start-line bias.

After checking the line try to get a transit between the buoy, the committee boat and a mark on land. If you can sight land then sail along the line away from it. Position yourself at the end of the start line and align the buoy and the committee boat with something such as a house or tree on the land. If you can do this you can then tell if you are over or below the line by simply glancing at your marker ashore. If you do get a good transit, check that the line isn't moved between your sighting and the five-minute gun.

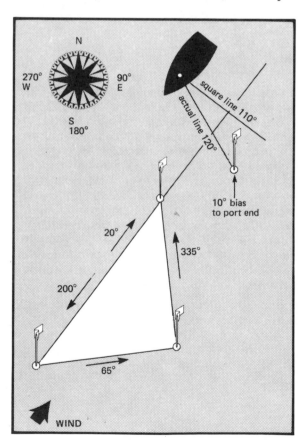

Pre-start manoeuvring. In light winds you can stay in position on starboard tack for up to two minutes before the start. To luff, pull the mainsheet in and ease the jib (top left); to bear away ease the main and back the jib (above). You can also reverse – pushing the boom out to port sends you backwards and also makes the boat bear away (left). Pushing the boom to starboard makes you luff as you reverse. Once you're moving backwards the tiller acts in reverse, i.e. push it to bear away.

At the ten-minute gun

Once the ten-minute gun has been fired all your pre-start work (other than checking the wind) must end. You must also have eaten your food, taken plenty of fluid, filled or emptied your weight jacket, and worked out all the bearings to each mark.

Do not now cruise up and down the line risking being hit by other 'cruisers'; Instead go to the end of the line which is favoured and check the wind to make sure it is falling into its predicted pattern. Try to sight your transit to make sure neither end has drifted, and then make your way to your chosen position on the line.

If the line is biased then you must start as close to the favoured end as possible. Make your mind up before the five-minute gun which end it is and decide that you are the one who is going to get the best start.

At the five-minute gun

You are now in the most critical five minutes of the race and there must be no mistakes. Check the wind for the last time and make sure your wind readings are all adding up to some sort of pattern. This is most important in an oscillating wind as it dictates your first tack. If at five minutes to go the wind is veered by 10° it will probably mean a 5° favour to the starboard end; this, however, won't be enough because after about ten minutes the wind may back 10° giving the port-end starters a 5° advantage; 5° at the port end would mean port-end starters crossing the fleet.

The port or pin-end start

Having decided to start at the port end, arrive 100 yards up from the buoy with two minutes to go. Stay as close to the line as possible (using your transit if you have one) without being over, and as near head to wind as possible without losing control. The best way to keep your boat head to wind is to raise your rudder blade 10° and every time your bow blows away from the wind, push your tiller hard down and 'paddle' the boat back into the wind. Your crew must hold both jib sheets ready to sheet or back the jib to control the angle of the boat. Sheeting the mainsail and easing the jib turns the boat into the wind, and easing the main and sheeting or backing the jib makes the boat bear away.

You must stay head to wind as you need to create space to leeward so that you can sail free and fast after the gun has gone. You will need, ideally, one boat length between yourself and the boat to leeward to ensure a good start. Any less will invariably mean the boat to leeward will force you into a lee-bow position. Any more is fine providing another boat reaching along behind the line doesn't fill the gap with 30 seconds to go.

All the time keep checking your position on the line by checking your transit or, if this is not possible, by keeping your bow in line with the bows of boats around you. If they go ahead, you go ahead. If they drop back you must drop back, all the time being aware of the risk of being picked out as the boat 'most' over the line. This often happens in big fleet starts where the whole fleet is over the line but the race officer lets the start go and picks out the boats that were further over than the pack. Don't, however, play too safe and drop back behind other boats as the gap in the line will close and you will start in the second or third rank.

Assuming you have created a gap of at least one boat length to leeward with 10 seconds to go, your boat must be slowly moving forward hard on the wind. With 5 seconds to go you must be moving fast enough to hit the line on the gun at full speed. Timing is all-important, and your position relative to boats around vital. If you go for speed too soon you will risk poking your bow ahead of boats around and

being disqualified. If you go too late you will be squeezed out by boats to leeward and windward and, within 10 seconds, be yards behind the fleet— then only lucky windshifts can save you from arriving at the first mark in the mid-fifties. Therefore if you are close to or even over the line, keep abreast of the boats to leeward and windward. The very second they sheet in their sails you must follow. As soon as the gun goes bear away slightly and try to sail over the boat to leeward. Once you are over and past her you have made an excellent start.

If, however, you don't manage to sail over the boat to leeward you must hold your distance from her. Providing the boat on your weather is not going past you it doesn't matter if the boat to leeward goes ahead as long as you can hold up and stay clear of her lee bow. Try to hold this position as long as possible while you begin to check your compass to decide if you are on the right tack for your wind-shift sequence. If you are on a lift then you must hold on; if not then tack as soon as you are clear.

The starboard-end start

Starting at the starboard end can be dangerous in that a bad start means you have to tack to clear your air. This immediately separates you from the rest of the fleet going off the line on starboard presumably on a lift (as the wind must have shifted between the race officer laying the line and the start, making it a starboard-biased line).

Therefore when starting at this end you must be able to keep clear air and stay on starboard waiting for the wind to back. The actual starting procedure is the same as for the port end, except that it is normally safer to stay to leeward of any bunch of boats fighting for pole position by the committee boat. If you do get boxed in by boats around, escape by sailing further down the line looking for a nice gap that someone skilful has created for you. You must, however, recognise very quickly the danger signs of a bad start and get out at least 45 seconds before the gun.

The gate start

Starting any race through a gate is, in itself, reasonably easy; the skill is deciding where to start. Other things (such as tide and wind) being equal, you should start early if you are faster than the pathfinder,

Above: a port-biased line start.

or late if she is faster than you. It is, however, very seldom that such options are open because invariably there are other factors to take into consideration.

Position relative to the fleet. Gate starts normally only happen in fleets of 100 or more. To start very early or late on an effective line of a quarter-mile could leave you in bad shape should the wind shift after the start. It is, therefore, good policy to start near the middle if you are confident of your boat's speed.

Apart from exceptional circumstances such as beating into stronger or weaker tide it is always the best strategy to start near the middle, get off the line and stay on starboard until you are clear to tack on any shifts without ducking behind other boats. If

you can do this you are automatically in the top third of the fleet due to other boats sailing in bad air and having to cross behind starboard tackers. From a gate start you can never tack for at least two minutes, so you must ensure a good start and wait to play the shifts until the fleet has spread. Therefore fleet and speed strategy, rather than wind strategy, are the key to the first beat. Once you are clear to tack, get into the wind pattern and try at all times to cover the majority of the fleet. This ploy, together with reasonable speed, should always get you around the first mark in the top ten.

Going through the gate. If you think it will pay to start late then go through the gate when two-thirds of the fleet have gone, and if you favour an early start, when one-third has gone. Try to go through with as few boats around you as possible and, as in line

505s making a gate start in San Francisco bay.

starts, you must create space to leeward on your start. To achieve this you must clip the stern of the gate launch going at full speed hard on the wind. Do not come down to the launch on a reach as when you round up you will lose distance to leeward and find yourself too close to the boat below.

If you do make a poor start and fall into bad air, your only option is to tack and bear away behind the other boats, going either all the way to the end of the gate, or tacking back in a space between starboard tackers. Depending on the wind, you may be lucky and get away into a reasonable position as you are only losing one boat length to each starboard boat, and usually you should be able to cross in front of slower boats or bad starters.

Finishing

Approaching the finish line, always aim to cross at the end of the line which would *not* be favoured were it a start line. In other words, as you are approaching the line imagine it to be the start and go for the opposite end to which you would start. Having decided which end is favoured, go for that end at full speed, just shaving either buoy or finish vessel. *Don't cross the line in the middle* as there is always a favoured end and you may lose places. If you are almost level with an opponent, then a final luff head to wind, seconds before your bow crosses the line, could decide the finishing order in your favour.

11 Conclusion

There are basically three components that establish the speed of a boat: (1) the helm and crew, (2) the sails and rig and (3) the hull shape. In order of importance the helm and crew are easily first, followed by sail and rig and then hull.

It is imperative, if you are to be in the top 10 per cent of a championship, that your boat is right. Always remember that yards matter and anything that can gain or lose ten yards is important. Therefore be sure that your hull is fair; it is pointless spending hours sanding rudder and centreboard if your slot rubbers are old and worn and your self-bailers do not fit flush with the hull.

Only have fittings that you understand fully and know how to use. For instance, some years ago it became the fashion to use shroud levers. Only about one sailor in ten really understood their purpose, and much thought was wasted during the race on the mysteries of shroud levers. Never slavishly follow fashion; make up your own mind whether or not a piece of equipment will help you to get better speed and if you will, in fact, use it. In most championship boat parks there is enough 'go fast' gear that doesn't add a yard to the speed of their owners' boats to fill a good-sized chandlery.

Make certain that all your gear is in first-class working order. A surprising number of boats have cleats that slip, blocks that won't turn, etc. Try a small squirt of WD40 on all your pulleys to make them run freely, and check and check again so that you can be sure nothing will break during the race.

Get your boat down to weight if possible, but don't get neurotic about it — 5 lb underweight or overweight never won or lost a championship. I have known people go to enormous lengths to bring a boat that is 5 lb over down to minimum weight, then arrive in the starting area two minutes before the ten-minute gun totally unprepared mentally and with a thick head from last night's beer.

Rigs today have become fairly sophisticated and the number of controls is sometimes bewildering. If you aspire to the top ten of a big fleet you must understand the use and interrelationship of various control and rig settings. For instance, spreader length and angle, kicker, mast ram and mainsheet all affect mast bend. Mast bend affects sail shape, the slot, genoa setting, and so on.

It is beyond the scope of this book to explain the black art of boat tuning, but learn as much as you can from people who know — not from people who think they know or say they know, but from people whose results make you *believe* they know. Everyone from beginners to world champions is always learning something different about rigs so no one can tell you everything, but learn as much as you can. Tuning a boat to win, like most things that bring success, is a painstaking process, and that elusive extra speed is unlikely to be gained by simply buying a new suit of sails for the championships, sticking them up for the first time for the practice race and hoping they will make you go faster.

Old sails seldom win races, but tune your boat to the new sails before you get to the championship, and don't buy an extreme suit that will be a winner in one set of conditions — get a suit that can be set up for all conditions by rig controls. Listen to your sailmaker, and beware of pet theories — your own or anyone else's. I have never seen a championship won with a suit of sails that was a 'design breakthrough'. Improvement in sail design is, again, a slow and painstaking process, so treat with suspicion the 'magic formula' man.

The important thing to remember is that the best hull and the best rig in the fleet will not win if the helm and crew are second rate, and the best helm and crew will not win if they are not properly prepared.

The only point in sailing is to get enjoyment and satisfaction — not always the same thing. Before you go to the championships decide if you are going for a 'jolly' and hope to do as well as you can without too much hassle, or if you really want to be as far up the fleet as possible. At least 50 per cent of a big fleet know, before the start of the first race, they have as much chance of finishing in the top ten as of winning the pools. These lads go for a good sail, good company, a good laugh and, usually, plenty of ale. They are the backbone of any class and, without them, there would be no championship — always remember this.

On the other hand, if you want to win you must be in top physical and mental shape for five or six hours a day for six days. So live quietly at the championships, go to bed early, get up early and prepare everything quietly and methodically so that you are not panicked into last-minute hitches.

Don't be discouraged by big reputations and by the people who seem to you unbeatable. If you, your crew and your boat are all properly prepared and your pre-race routine is correct, if you keep clear of protests and you are a good club helmsman, you are almost sure of a place in the top 20 per cent. Don't let one bad result, a disastrous start or a slow boat passing you put you off. There is a lot of sailing in a week's championship and fortunes ebb and flow like the tide. It is amazing how fortunes fluctuate during six or seven races.

At almost every championship one of the fancied competitors spoils his chances by a stupid mistake. Make sure you *know* the course (sometimes race officers do the unexpected). Don't forget tallies and five-minute rules. Take all the gear out you will need: some years ago an Olympic helmsman sailed a championship race without a spinnaker pole — he had inadvertently left it ashore!

Respect your fellow competitors — especially the lads down the fleet — don't get drawn into private feuds, and avoid trouble like the plague — it destroys your composure and balance and ruins your concentration. If you are involved in an incident, put up your protest flag and then forget it until you are ashore — don't get involved in acrimony during the race.

Finally — sail hard, sail to win, keep a sense of proportion at all times . . . and enjoy yourself.

Good luck!